NANCY RAINES DAY

illustrated by KURT CYRUS

What IN THE World?

Numbers in Nature

BEACH LANE BOOKS • New York   London   Toronto   Sydney   New Delhi

What in the world comes one by one?

A nose.

A mouth.

The moon.

The sun.

What in the world comes two by two?

A pair of birds with wings of blue.

What in the world comes grouped in threes?

Leaves of a clover, bodies of bees.

What in the world
comes four by four?

Petals of poppies, hooves—and more.

What in the world comes five by five?

The arms of sea stars, all alive.

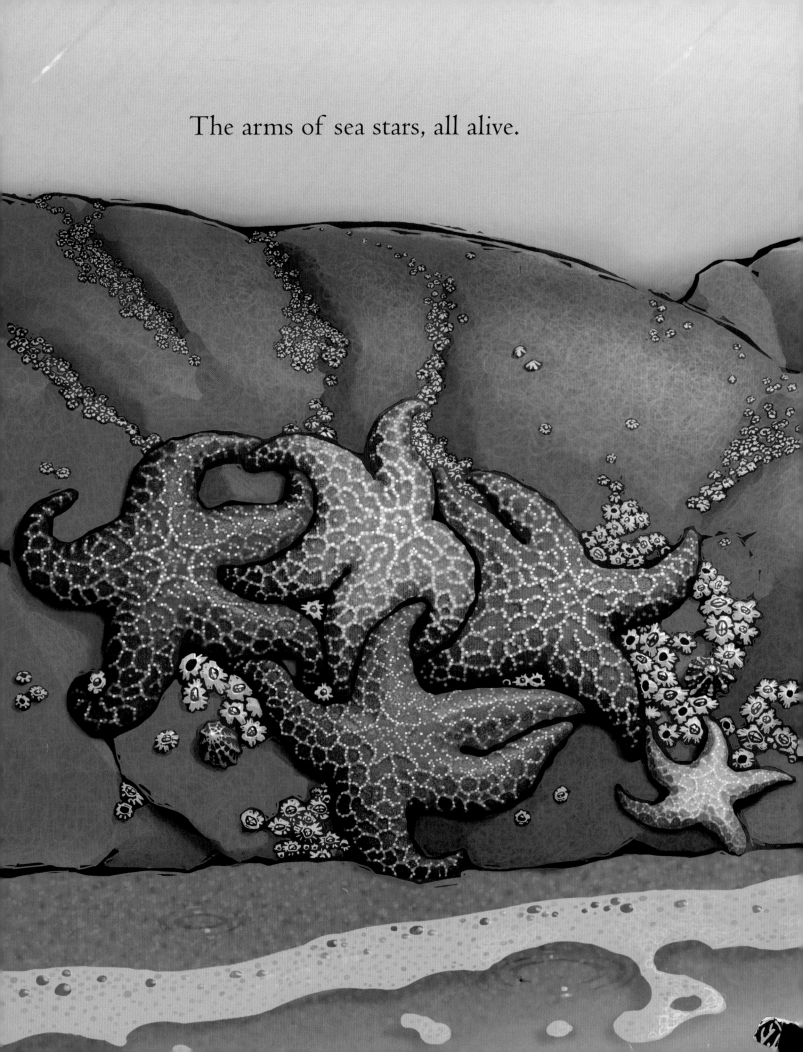

What in the world comes six by six?

The twiggy legs of walking sticks.

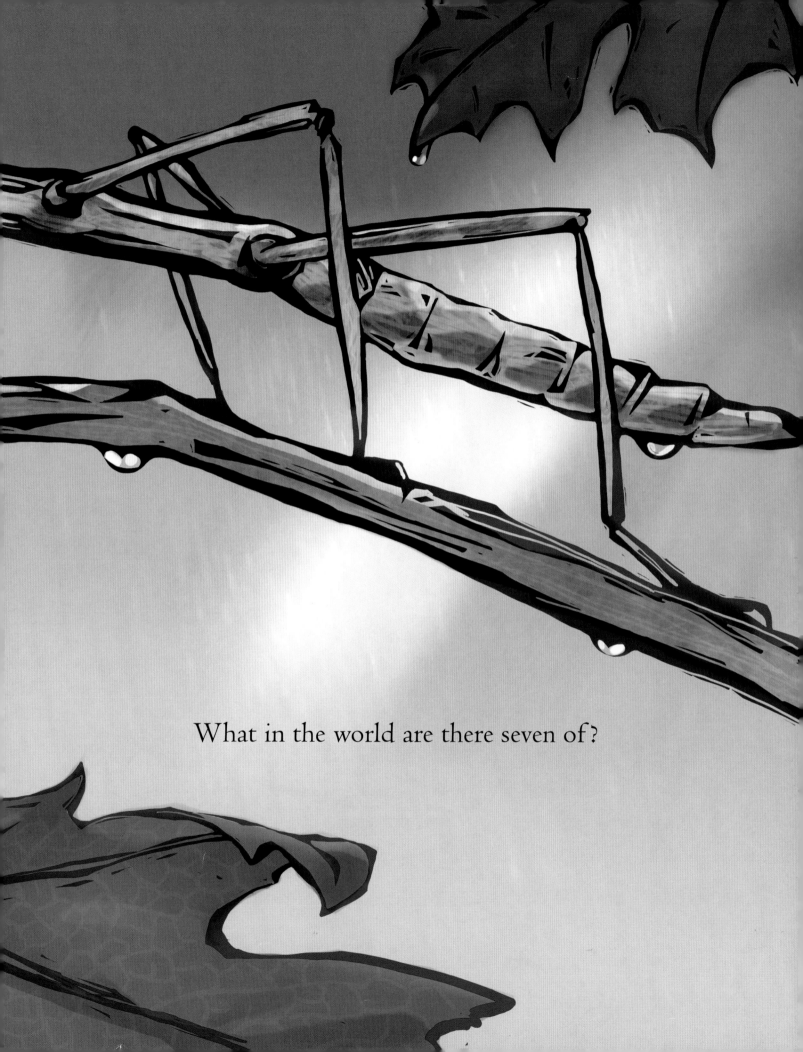

What in the world are there seven of?

Colors in rainbows arched above.

What in the world comes eight by eight?

Octopus limbs that undulate.

What in the world comes grouped in nines?

Stickleback fish's prickly spines.

What in the world comes ten by ten?

Fingers and toes that wiggle and bend.

And what comes in sets too big to count?

Stars in the sky—

a vast amount!

Author's Note

A numerical set is a group of similar things that occur together. A bird has two wings, a small set. Humans have ten fingers, a bigger set. The night sky has too many stars to count—the biggest set in this book.

Look for a numerical set in the world around you. How many things come in this set? See how many sets you can find!

To McKenna and Ava with worlds of love—N. R. D.

Beach Lane Books
An imprint of Simon & Schuster Children's Publishing Division
1230 Avenue of the Americas, New York, New York 10020
Text copyright © 2015 by Nancy Raines Day • Illustrations copyright © 2015 by Kurt Cyrus
All rights reserved, including the right of reproduction in whole or in part in any form.
Beach Lane Books is a trademark of Simon & Schuster, Inc.
For information about special discounts for bulk purchases, please contact Simon & Schuster Special Sales
at 1-866-506-1949 or business@simonandschuster.com.
The Simon & Schuster Speakers Bureau can bring authors to your live event. For more information or to book an event,
contact the Simon & Schuster Speakers Bureau at 1-866-248-3049 or visit our website at www.simonspeakers.com.
Book design by Lauren Rille • The text for this book is set in Centaur. • The illustrations for this book are drawn and colored digitally.
Manufactured in China • 0615 SCP • First Edition • 10 9 8 7 6 5 4 3 2 1
Library of Congress Cataloging-in-Publication Data
Day, Nancy Raines, author.
What in the world? : numbers in nature / Nancy Raines Day ; Illustrated by Kurt Cyrus.—First edition. • p. cm.
Summary: "A rhyming nonfiction picture book that explores the numerical sets—'two birds, eight octopus arms, ten fingers and toes, etc.'—
that occur throughout the natural world."—Provided by publisher.
Audience: Ages 4–8. • Audience: K to grade 3.
ISBN 978-1-4814-0060-2 (hardcover) • ISBN 978-1-4814-0061-9 (eBook)
1. Counting—Juvenile literature. 2. Natural history—Juvenile literature. 3. Set theory—Juvenile literature. I. Cyrus,
Kurt, illustrator. II. Title.
QA113.D39 2015 • 513.5—dc23 • 2014008218